Rhymes of the Newfangled Mariner

Poems by Dick Dixon

Drawings by Reine Mazoyer

Mereo Books

2nd Floor, 6-8 Dyer Street, Cirencester, Gloucestershire, GL7 2PF
An imprint of Memoirs Books. www.mereobooks.com
and www.memoirsbooks.co.uk

Rhymes of the Newfangled Mariner
978-1-86151-350-2

First published in Great Britain in 2016

© Poems - Dick Dixon
© Illustrations - Reine Mazoyer

Copyright ©2021

Dick Dixon has asserted his right under the Copyright Designs and Patents Act 1988 to be identified as the author of this work.

Reine Mazoyer asserts her right to be identified as the author of the illustrations.

A CIP catalogue record for this book is available from the British Library.
This book is sold subject to the condition that it shall not by way of trade or otherwise be lent, resold, hired out or otherwise circulated without the publisher's prior consent in any form of binding or cover, other than that in which it is published and without a similar condition, including this condition being imposed on the subsequent purchaser.

The address for Memoirs Books can be found at www.mereobooks.com

Mereo Books Ltd. Reg. No. 12157152

Contents

1	Is Susan Sad?	1	07/12/14
2	The Escape	3	28/03/15
3	The Conversation	7	27/10/14
4	Old Men	9	26/06/15
5	Snoring Dogs	11	28/05/15
6	The Wicked	13	26/04/15
7	Fishy Friends	15	28/03/16
8	A Question Of Water	19	17/01/16
9	The Elephant In The Room	23	17/05/16
10	Dressing Up	25	03/05/15
11	The Running Of The Bath	28	03/01/16
12	Elephants In The Bush	33	26/05/16
13	In Praise Of Frogmen	35	16/05/15
14	Medical Advice	39	27/04/15
15	Skeletons In The Cupboard	41	30/06/16
16	What Is It?	45	11/07/15
17	Three Towns	49	23/06/15
18	Home, Sweet Home	53	01/01/16
19	Exclusive Dining Club	55	27/12/15
20	In The Wood	59	10/07/15
21	Empty Space	61	30/12/15
22	Berkeley Square	63	20/06/15
23	The Power Of Prayer	67	07/05/16
24	Descartes' Twin	71	05/04/16
25	Hospital Visit	73	15/05/16
26	Steambergs	78	25/06/15
27	The Possibilities	81	14/03/16
28	When I Am Gone	83	01/05/16
29	Wise Old Birds	85	19/12/15
30	Flowers	89	26/06/15
31	Brooklyn	92	17/03/15

Preface

Following hard on the heels of 'Rhymes for no Reason', our earlier volume of odd reflections in a distorted mirror, we now seem to have written a new one, entitled 'Rhymes of the Newfangled Mariner'. We do not intend any disrespect to S.T. Coleridge of course, author of the famous poem, as it seems only right to acknowledge his celebrated nautical account. In his case however, he was dealing with an ancient mariner, while in ours, the Mariner is decidedly modern in his quayside approach, as one might term it. For one thing, there is no creature in the entire book which comes within striking distance of a boat or ship, though it may be regarded as a close-run thing in 'A Question of Water' for example. Accordingly, the book is somewhat consistent with the modern concept of Doublethink, which may be considered a constituent part of Newspeak, as described so aptly by George Orwell. 'Saying it makes it so', and why on earth, or on sea, would we want to intervene with the truth when there is a good story to be had! Thus the 'Newfangled Mariner' wanders languidly through the pages, inviting recognition from you and gently chiding when you do not join in the game with the required gusto. As you encounter each new poem, you should simply utter the mantra: 'I recognise and applaud you as the Newfangled Mariner I seek in order to assist and reassure me throughout the passage that is this life'. The Mariner will retreat, satisfied, and sail on. I cannot guarantee your complete safety if you neglect to execute this simple precaution.

Even if you are unable to recognise the itinerant Mariner as he passes mistily through the paper and ink, at least you will be able to take comfort that he travels not in solitude. His constant lady companion, who is not a Martinet, nor a Marchioness, nor even a Marinade, though perhaps she might be dubbed a Marinette, is able to supply encouragement and support, and also the odd Martini perhaps, to sustain them as they voyage though the salt-stained pages.

Within these very pages, you can hope, and what a vain hope it will be I'm afraid, to find a little light cast upon a few of the many problems that beset each one of us as we pursue our own various journeys through the strange experience that we call life.

(This light is cast in verse form of course, and also in a series of brilliant illustrations in full colour, one for each poem, by Reine Mazoyer, the well-known French artist who also illustrated 'Rhymes for no Reason'. It does seem that Reine has captured the essence perfectly in every case, and these illustrations will themselves provide endless scope for study).

For example, might it be possible to leave planet earth on a more or less permanent basis, and where should one aim for, if so? On the other hand, if one should decide to stay, is it feasible to become an alternative form of life, if that is considered necessary?

Then again, what should one do about one's skeletons in the cupboard, if there are any, and what options are there if an elephant should present itself in a room where you had believed yourself to be the sole occupant?

A few examples of other topics examined are: the role of religion in mitigating the risk of being consumed by cannibals, and the question of how global warming might be controlled by observing the habits of certain animal species.

There are several other situations that I do hope will be made less terrifying or mystifying by the consideration of the words within, and I would like to take this opportunity to apologise in advance if the desired level or reassurance or comfort is somehow not attained.

Do try if you can to find something here to help you in your own voyage through the oceans of your life, whether they be choppy or calm - for I fear that you may not get a second chance!

Bon voyage!!

Dick Dixon...........3/9/16.

Rhymes of the Newfangled Mariner

Is Susan Sad?

'Can the reason why Susan seems so sad,
Be that her upper storey needs a tad
Of help to boost her assets more,
So she can show the world the door?
(As many of the bras she's tried
Will only fit two eggs, both fried!)'.

'She really must consult a doc,
Who's got a plan you'd call ad hoc,
To bring her closer to her wish:
A dreamy and delicious dish'.

"Well that is just what she has done;
He's charmed her with some silicone,
To make her prospects large and pointed,
With sequins, tassels and double-jointed!"

"No more fried eggs for Susan's lunch;
What she's got now packs far more punch.
I expect that there's enough for all;
Enough to fill the Albert Hall!"

––––––––––––––––––

Now Sue can hold her head up high;
She must, you know — it's that or die
Of suffocation (or something worse).
So beware, beware the surgeon's curse:
When you decide to change your luck,
Make sure it's just a nip and tuck.

The Escape

It's hell here on earth,
As we can all see,
So surely there's somewhere
It's better to be.

Mars can be chilly,
And mountainous too;
Mercury's boiling,
And there isn't a loo.

Jupiter's hefty,
With plenty of room,
But lacking in night life,
And frozen in gloom.

Ceres has water,
Which is a rare treat,
But the shops are all shut,
So there's nothing to eat.

Venus sounds brilliant,
If you want to be flat;
Its air is so heavy,
You'd soon go ker-splat!

Saturn's so lovely
At this time of year,
But the rings make you dizzy,
And there's no decent beer.

Uranus is fun,
If you say it just right;
The appeal though wears off,
And there isn't much light.

Neptune could be fine:
The solution to this —
If poisonous gases
You don't want to miss!

Pluto's minute, and
Incredibly cold,
And when you arrive,
You find you're too old.

Then there's the moon,
So silver and small,
But hardly the place
For a game of football.

We mustn't give up though,
Our quest without fight —
We could go to the sun,
Which is well in our sight.

You think it's too fiery,
Too hot and too bright?
Well don't fret about that;
We can just go at night!

The Conversation

People say, though not to me,
How much they would prefer to be
In a Turkish jail today;
At least I think that's what they say —
Or duelling with an octopus,
Or dodging hailstones while at sea,
After long and painful dentistry,
Or simply getting on a bus,
To take them far from here, you see.

They'll say to me our chats don't pall;
They'd love to talk more in the hall —
They wonder though who'll feed the dog,
With earnest frown, and all agog.
It's such a gripping subject too!
They'll say I had them in my thrall;
Perhaps tomorrow they might call?
I say of course, and so would you,
How much I'll miss them — warts and all!

Old Men

An old man remembers;
An older one forgets
How gilded youth came once and went,
How once straight tree trunks now are bent,
And hair that once could grace a prince,
Has been reduced to fronds and wisps.

An old man remembers;
An older one regrets
That hours cannot retrace their path,
As water will not fill a bath
Until the taps and plug are wet,
And in unholy marriage set.

An old man remembers;
An older one's secrets
May never see the light of day,
In Antioch or Bantry Bay.
Some things are better not released,
And in particular, this beast!

Snoring Dogs

Never ask a snoring dog
Its name or date of birth,
Or any other juicy facts,
About perhaps its weight or girth,
As lady-dogs may not regard
Such questions with much mirth!

It's most unlikely that you'll get
A woof or snort that's worth
Receiving, as we surely know
That even if we comprehend
The complex canine code
They seem to send —
Well, just forget it, as
It'll only leave you asking 'why?'

The truth is that a dog whose
Eyes are firmly closed, won't often try
To tell it as it is, because —
Frankly, some dogs are rather sly
And like to lead you far astray
I s'pose; but then, we didn't poke or pry,
Criticize, or disapprove, — just gazed,
Just rolled our eyes towards the sky,
And were complicit in their ways.
We just let sleeping dogs lie.

The Wicked

No piece for the wicked,
No slice for the sinner,
No quarter for the quisling,
And for the damned — no dinner!

Fishy Friends

Did I ever say I'd seen
A haddock on a bike of green,
Riding bravely through the rain,
Perhaps to catch the morning train,
Grappling with the handlebars,
To steer well clear of vans and cars?
A symphony of tail and fin,
Of cool red blood and scaly skin,
No doubt at all, he was the king,
With head held high and 'quite the thing'.

And did I say he met a friend,
In trouble on an uphill bend?
It was a lobster on a scooter,
But clearly with a failing hooter.
The gears were also quite a trial,
And lobsters suffer from denial —
'How best to help?' I hear you ask,
(I must agree, it's quite a task!);
But haddocks have a wisdom rare,
And always render utmost care.

Here the answer was quite clear,
Even if the lobster's ear
Was not completely tuned to hear
How he might allay his fear —
Delivered by a cycling fish —
Not perhaps all he might wish.
Their kinship after all is slight,
But 'needs must' at times, to put things right.
Help should not be turned away,
Otherwise we'd need to pray!

Thus the cycling haddock told:
'Perhaps my plan is rather bold,
But surely you should now dismount,
And put your claws upon the ground.
Your many legs you can disport,
So have no need of wheeled transport'.
The lobster took the news with glee:
"I'm so glad you're here with me.
I never would have thought of that.
I'll give my scooter to a water rat".

A Question Of Water

Do you have a blackened toe,
Or several cuts that will not heal?
Perhaps you find it hard to go,
And look at life without much zeal.

What about your coated tongue,
Or cracking joints that scare the cat?
Then again, though spring has sprung,
Why does it all seem — oh so flat?

After all, you're not so old,
Fifty-two, I think you said;
Time to be a little bold:
At least — get up from that old bed!

All you need, I have to say,
A pick-me-up will soon supply.
Let me ring the doc today:
Those eyes of yours will soon be dry!

Oh, did you say — the bed is damp,
But not from tears in your distress?
That anyway, you must decamp:
'Twas too much tea, and laziness?

And do not bother with the doc?
There is no special need for him?
In it I should put a sock,
And just float off and fetch some gin?

I think not, my bed-bound friend;
Time for us to now depart —
To East Sussex we must wend,
Where they're versed in much black art!

> To Eastbourne, where they leak, and sway,
> Though cures there are, with your consent,
> But not that place with boats — no way,
> As Newhaven's for the continent!

PS   I feel that I should point out to readers that the fine town of Eastbourne was celebrated, in the recent past at least, for its considerable elderly population, many of whom were receiving medical attention for a variety of ailments that such citizens are liable to suffer from. The neighbouring town of Newhaven is a place from which it is possible to travel to France by crossing the English Channel by boat or ferry.

The Elephant In The Room

The elephant in the room
Has gone for a walk;
Well, you can't coop them up in the house!
He just rose from the floor,
Sucked open the door,
And squeezed out, just like a mouse.

The elephant in the room
Has left a vast space;
I shall miss his great trunk before long.
I hope he's not lost,
Or peppered with frost,
And nobody sees that he's gone.

The elephant in the room
Is worrying me;
How could I have let him escape?
The neighbours will moan,
And play hell on the phone;
In extremis, I must crush a grape!

The elephant in the room
Is not my concern,
It has suddenly occurred to me now.
Though inviting attention,
Never once was he mentioned,
So why would he furrow my brow?

Dressing Up

I must admit,
In times of stress,
I often need
To wear a dress.

At other times,
Sometimes all day,
I feel that jeans
Get in the way.

When people see
Me in the street,
I say, 'hello' ;
They say, 'how neat!'

What they feel though,
Is hard to say.
Maybe it's envy;
Perhaps they pray!

I don't care much —
It's quite common;
After all, I
Am a woman!

Reader — please note that the above was written by a friend of mine, who wishes to remain nameless.

The Running Of The Bath

My cousin Prue lay half-askew,
Her long legs on display;
'A foamy bath will meet my need',
Said she, at close of day.

The water gushed from golden taps,
And rose to fill the space
Between the two sides of the tub —
Then Prue slipped in with grace.

Prue lay back and breathed in steam,
Enveloped by hot water,
Which lapped around her creamy neck,
Then subsided as it ought to.

Soon after, in this perfect pond —
Though no ducks deigned to swim,
The water danced and rocked about,
And sloshed around the brim.

'Whatever's this?', Prue cried aloud,
'Quakes never come to Dover;
I need to scrub my many parts,
And some of them twice over!'

'But how can I in a tilting bath?
I must secure the plug —
Otherwise 'twill be a case of
Glug, glug, glug, glug, glug!'

But things soon went from bad to worse:
The bathroom door swung open,
And bath and Prue, and water too,
Shot forth in rapid motion.

Through the door and down the hall,
They sped in close alliance,
Then through the open door in front,
Which had yawned its clear defiance!

On to the street they bowled along,
With no sign yet of slowing,
As Prue in horror covered up
The parts she now was showing —

Though they had not been scrubbed twice,
Nor even once, in some odd bits,
But men, on foot and bikes still waved,
And called, which really was the pits!

Right arm poised — in her defence,
Prue rose to cast a nervous glance
Over the rim of the errant bath,
To see what made it buck and prance.

The sight she saw surprised and
Shocked her psyche to its socks;
The dreadful truth became quite clear,
As they hastened to the docks.

Four squat and hairy legs sat
At the corners of the vessel,
As replacements for the usual ones,
Which were really not so special.

'What to do?', thought mobile Prue,
'It's true indeed I'm quite a dame —
But no way can I go off today,
Without clothing to my name!'.

Just then a clap of thunder roared,
White lightning forks consumed a tree,
As Prue awoke in a tub quite dry,
Admired by all who'd come to see.

Elephants In The Bush

The elephant in the room,
Let's agree about this, is
Worth two in the proverbial bush,
Though it rather depends,
I suppose, in the end,
How hard you are able to push!

After all, it's quite far
From the veldt and savannah,
Of Africa's wildest retreat,
To your bedroom in Ealing,
With the reinforced ceiling,
And floor of the finest concrete.

I have a strong feeling,
That when all's said and done,
You are better off leaving things be;
You are bound to do better,
With a jumbo that's fettered,
And one that you don't need to feed!

In Praise Of Frogmen

It's most important to a frog
To leap from place to place:
You should see his shining face
When little legs are flexed at speed,
From normal gravity he's freed,
And he launches into space.

I'd often watched this great display,
And wondered how he did it.
It was so cool to — ribit —
Ribit to his heart's content,
And in my mind some nagging bent
Would not let go, I do admit.

I felt some kinship with this chap;
No longer could I sit and wait —
I would have to be his mate.
I made a list of things to do,
To approximate a kangaroo —
More my size at any rate!

Time to ditch the steak and chips,
And all those ice-cream cornets,
And listen well, without regrets
To my body's clarion call:
Did I not regard at all
Its need for crunchy hornets?

Let me tell you here and now:
There is no need to make a fuss;
My open jaws would catch a bus,
So snaring flies is quite a breeze,
While wasps and bees are caught with ease,
Though the stings do make me cuss!

After several years of this,
Of ants and bugs and chrysalids,
Of feasts at dawn on green aphids,
And leaping practice every morn,
With friend Pierre, a displaced prawn,
I've really no more need for kids.

Pierre just sits, all quiet and pink,
To watch me from the water's edge,
As I scale with ease the garden hedge;
Or in a pensive mood, just soak,
And emit a low, contented croak,
Amid the lily-pads and sedge.

The other thing I ought to say:
How well my lovely body's coped;
In fact it's almost all I'd hoped.
Now my legs are green and cool —
I often sport them by the pool,
And now of course, no need for soap.

My skin as well is rather fine;
It has a wondrous olive hue,
Chock-full of brilliant spots — it's true.
But one last problem still remains,
In this odd life of loss and gains:
I'm still a frog of six-foot two!

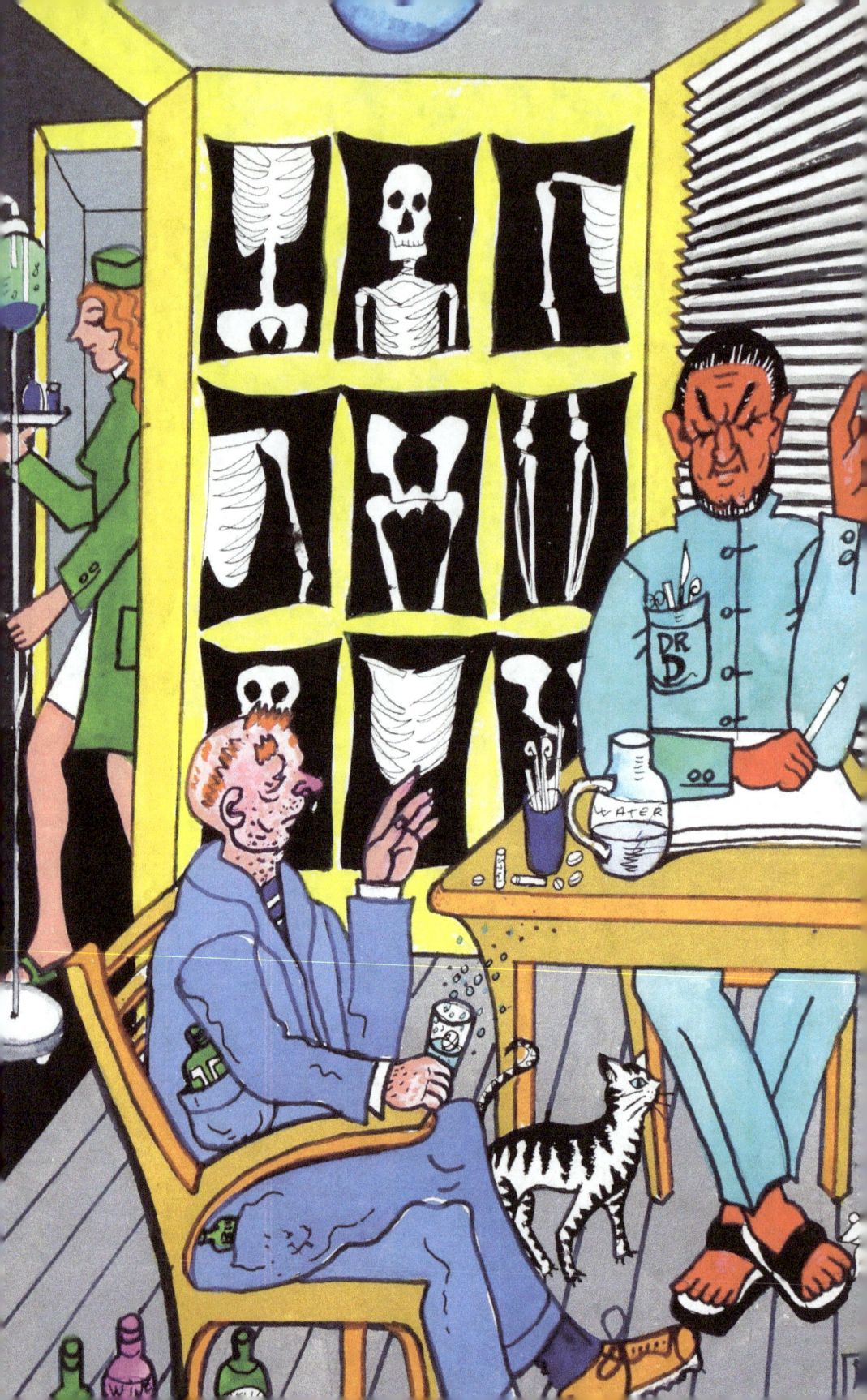

Medical Advice

'Do not exceed the stated dose!'
It's bound to make you more morose;
You must trust your friendly doc
To get it right, and should not mock
His vain attempts to diagnose
The reason for your purple nose.

He will tell you — no doubt here,
To lay off whisky, wine and beer,
Even though you're 'mostly dry'
You say without the blinking eye!
Anyway, you have the pills —
Three a day, and no cheap thrills;
More's not better, as we know,
And four is where we must not go.
'Do not exceed the stated dose'
Is as plain as your ten toes.

But what he maybe doesn't say
Is: one's enough to wreck your day.
In that case take drink and pill,
Then wait a bit, and then you will,
See them both again 'tout de suite',
All upon your tiny feet!

PS. For those whom it may concern: These are intended to be a few reflections on the use and abuse of 'Antabuse'. Perhaps you have never heard of it, lucky old you!

Skeletons In The Cupboard

Skeletons in the cupboard
Should look before they leap,
Especially if the cupboard door is closed,
As it's hard to find the way,
In the blackness of the fray,
As they risk the hanging columns full of clothes.

Then the flight itself is fraught,
If two crashing skulls report,
As the metal hangers clang and swing and slide,
And traversing dusty dressers
In the dark, daunts and depresses,
Though it must be done, or at the least be tried.

As even though they're bony,
There's really nothing phoney,
About a skelly's pressing need to exercise:
They're coiled and ultra-frisky,
Though it's really rather risky,
As they'll never know when someone needs some tights!

You may not have considered
A skeleton's emotions,
But he worries just as much as you or I,
That a sedentary state,
Will lead to gain in weight,
And loss of mental sharpness, by and by.

A soupçon of discretion
Will also be in order,
If I tell you what a skelly-gent likes most:
It's a skelly-girl who's trim,
In the cupboard space with him,
When they leap together, after tea and toast.

May I ask you then in earnest:
If your need's for satin garters,
Or even bras and knickers for your bride,
Please listen and don't grumble
At the rumble in your jumble;
Just wait until it's quiet again inside!

What Is It?

It's round and flat,
With a hole in the middle.
It's not worth much —
In fact very little.

Some people say
They'd rather ignore
Such a small thing,
As it's rather a bore.

They really don't like it,
Around or about —
And say when they see it,
They feel they could shout.

But oh, let's be careful,
Before we take aim,
To blast the poor thing;
It would be such a shame.

The fact is: we need it;
Without it we're sunk.
We mustn't believe those
Who talk so much bunk.

It's really quite easy
For you to foretell,
The difference between
Sweet heaven and hell.

And it's just like that here,
And easily done,
To distinguish between
A ten and a one.

As long as you have
Our little flat friend,
Who goes round in circles,
And so round the bend.

You see what I mean?
It's easy you know,
As all you will need
Is a big fat zero!

PS Our friend is big as well as little, and fat as well as flat!

Three Towns

In Mashem, Basham and Cosham,
They'll fight at the drop of a hat.
You don't need to give 'em a reason:
Just stand there — they'll pummel you flat!

In Basham and Cosham it's normal;
They're proud of their pugilists, see!
They really don't like to be formal —
They'd rather see you in a tree!

Some people say it's the water,
Though others are sure it's the diet,
But whatever the cause of the slaughter,
They would certainly like you to try it!

It's rather different in Mashem,
Though in some ways exactly the same;
They'll still make you fear and respect 'em,
As bashing and coshing's their game.

But in Mashem they're subtle about it;
They don't like to warn you before.
One moment you feel you could wing it —
The next: dripping blood on the floor!

In Mashem they used to be stressing,
That people wouldn't come to a town,
Whose name suggested a mashing
Might bring them right down to the ground.

So to get more business they changed it,
To sound not like 'mash', but like 'medz'.
That way, people still come and visit —
Just once, then it's off with their heads!

(With profound apologies to the people of Cosham, who are, by and large, very nice people. The other two places are located in a country that it is wiser not to visit).

Home, Sweet Home

'What think you now, dear friend of mine?
Do tell me how you feel;
I consider that you really ought
To have another meal'.

'Life in your home is maybe not
Much joy, I comprehend:
You've been there now for three full months,
And show no wish to wend'.

"I'm waiting for the turnip time,
When passions rise so high,
And crowds of stars repopulate
The fulminating sky".

"When echoes of the dawn retell
The story-book of old,
An ancient tale whose end has yet
To find its proper mould".

"For every action on this earth,
A price must sore be paid,
Unless ordained by nature's writ,
Which justifies its grade".

"And though I shall in time decamp,
And seek some nourishment,
The trine of Mars and Venus
Must appear by due consent."

"Though for the moment I may starve,
I'll hold fast to this trail:
I will be slimmer, and may I say,
A rather intellectual snail."

Exclusive Dining Club

There are those
Who wish to make a soup,
Or maybe chops,
Or casseroles galore,
From meat not found in normal shops,
Except perhaps a very special store.

Such meals are
Highly prized by some,
Who'll travel miles
On horseback for their lunch,
Though clearly worth it, for their smiles
Tell you oh so much about this hungry bunch.

Versed in Keats
Or Byron they are not;
Those may as well
Be awful tommy-rot —
As for dear Chopin: bloody hell!
He hardly rates a tittle, nor a jot!

And yet, to
See them at their work,
There's no doubt that
They're skilled in other arts:
Their ways of dealing with the fat,
Are equal to their cleaving of the parts.

Parts that is,
Of pastors in a pot,
Who boil away
And steam for hours to come;
Those poor chaps who'd meant to have their say,
Are now reduced to gristle, bone and gum.

Not to speak
Of tender chunks of steak:
The cuts of choice
Of woaded native types;
Full of meat, they scarcely make a noise,
Nor can they raise a match to light their pipes.

Divine one,
Where are you in our time
Of greatest need,
Our saddest, darkest hour?
Do implore your angels now to read
The riot act, to fight this evil power!

Send a seraph,
And winged cherubim, four-faced,
For the fearsome
Fight that falls across this day,
And as they rally to the drum,
Let flashing wings and firestorm there hold sway.

Man-eating
Men might see their few last hours,
And cause us not
More anger, nor distress;
Your wrath will no doubt vaporise their pots,
And the seraph can have cannibals for lunch,
with cress.

In The Wood

I believe in monogamy,
Although it's quite a wood,
With trees and twisting paths,
And echoes trapped in jars,
While far above, the stars
Gaze down upon the good.

Some prefer polygamy,
Another kind of wood:
Hall of sharpened splinters,
Dark and swirling rivers,
And endless frozen shivers;
I don't know how they could.

Yet others travel through
In violet-scented woods,
Searching for a kiss,
Thinking otherwise of this,
To find another kind of bliss,
Of colours, shapes and moods.

Empty Space

The atom's mostly empty space,
And that means you are too;
You're not the man you thought you were,
Just smoke and steam and glue.

If life has nothing for you,
And death does not appeal,
Console yourself that really,
Neither one of them is real.

Berkeley Square

A nightingale sang in Berkeley Square,
To the sinking sun, and the air,
And all down Park Lane,
The birds and the bees
Sat in the quiet trees,
And listened again and again
To his perfect refrain.

But something was odd in Berkeley Square,
Not the sinking sun or the air;
No, the strangeness of that
Was the bees and the birds
That gathered in herds,
That knew with the cats, and the bats
That he sang in E flat.

But for the birdsong in Berkeley Square,
Only stillness and solitude there:
No time could be told,
No word on the breeze,
Nor rustle of leaves
From the trees in the evening gold —
In one of those days of old.

The moon rose high over Berkeley Square,
So silent and silver and spare,
As the nightingale's song,
Sung with infinite care,
Seemed to offer a prayer
For those who had waited so long —
That their love might be blessed and strong.

Darkness fell soon upon Berkeley Square;
The moon cast her spell on those there,
And a chill sliced the air,
As the birds and the bees
Perched in the black trees,
To hear, so bizarre and so rare:
'A Nightingale Sang in Berkeley Square'.

The Power Of Prayer

What shall I do?
It's hard to say;
It's driving me insane.
What can I do?
I wish I knew —
It's a circular refrain.

The sky's dark red,
The grass pale brown,
The trees and bushes white;
In frost their bed,
And overhead,
A tangled mass of spite.

Now comes a gale,
A swirling wind
Of choking frozen dust;
This poisoned vale,
Once fit and hale,
Now makes me fear the worst.

I wish I could
Say where I was;
It seems as not before,
Though all the wood
That grows, is good —
But green and much too raw.

The sky, she says
It's much too late,
To learn what we forgot.
Too late, she says,
The dying rays
Are all we've bloody got!

No time now,
The wood's too new;
All that's left is prayer,
And it looks as though
We'll soon have snow,
To fill the freezing air.

I dream of youth;
There was time then,
Time and worlds to spare,
And love and warmth
With lovely Ruth —
How I wish I'd cared!

All the King's men
Signed up this day,
Could save a dying Queen,
With sword or pen,
From swamp or glen —
Yet fail this final scene.

So I stand here,
On this last day,
As stars now dim and fade,
And all I have are
A broken mirror,
And a cross I've not yet made.

Descartes' Twin   (or Cartesian Dualism).

My twin's René — he's quite well-known;
His fame's spread far and wide,
But sadly his opinion of
Himself he keeps inside.

Not even sure if he is real,
He frets away the hours
In thought — he rarely has a meal,
And builds strange mental towers.
He mutters at the empty walls
And weeps at setting suns;
He sometimes sleeps while standing up —
I think his time has run.
I've never understood him and
I'm sure he's barking mad,
But even though he has a screw
That's loose, he's not that bad;
Do you mind though if I ask you
A question — simply this:

If I invite you home with us,
For tea with cakes and jam,
Am I the one you'd rather ask
To pour? I think maybe I am!

PS Please keep all this quiet. Nobody knows I exist.

Hospital Visit

"You won't recall your father dear;
You died before he was born,
But I still see him on his horse,
As he rode around the lawn.

I can see his large pink head,
With teeth, in truth askew,
His heart so full of reddish blood,
Transfused at London Zoo.

His drink of choice was mercury,
With brandy for the nerves;
He always said it gave him strength,
And marshalled his reserves.

As in his heart a rage did burn,
So hot it harmed the horse,
Which often stopped abruptly just
Before the flaming gorse.

When he was born, he said to me,
What a lucky thing it was,
That he had come to save the world,
From all its sins, because —

Forgive me dear; I dropped off there,
But I know you have to go,
And hard it is to speak this way
Of your uncle, don't you know.

You mustn't go before you've had
Tea and cakes for the bride —
For any nephew that I have,
Is a colossus who bestrides —

The world itself, with ills to boot,
And when the call of duty comes,
Attacks the problem at its root:
Now the kettle's full of crumbs!

But shake it out: it's what it needs,
You are the man for the job,
Unless I have, with some regret,
Just heard your stifled sobs.

We are from a line of men,
Of knights, and barons gay;
Mere crumbs can never interfere,
While I am Queen of the May.

So kindly find my parasol,
While we wonder, wait and watch,
Then work anew, the world to save;
Please help yourself to Scotch.

But as we start our task my dear,
And the sun begins to sink,
There is something I must tell you,
Though not what you might think.

I had a visitor today,
About your height and weight;
He sat in silence in your chair,
Until it was quite late.

I would have liked to know him
Much better I think, because
He did seem rather nice, I thought —
But I wonder who he was."

PS. The reader may like to know that the foregoing represents in some essential respects, a conversation that the present author had with one of his aunts, as she approached the age of 90. The author at the time was a mere child of 48.

Steambergs

Icebergs once did cruise along in peace;
In plain sight they thronged the arctic bar,
Not living, but creeping without cease,
For centuries, beneath a golden star.

Time has passed and we must think anew:
Dark forces have conspired to change the scene;
The old ways now must alter through and through,
Or the future will not be as it has been.

Would you wish to see the rising tide,
And ever hotter climates bind the earth,
As polar ice shuns measure in its stride,
And icebergs to new water now give birth?

It's possible to see much further out,
A planet that is governed by the erg,
Where no one lives to hear your passioned shout,
When icebergs in a trice become steambergs.

The Possibilities

The possibilities are endless,
Unlike a piece of string,
Unless the ends are neatly joined:
A wedding with no ring,
Nor bride, nor groom, nor priest,
Nor any other earthly thing
But cold and empty air enclosed within —
Perhaps a breath of early spring.
But yes I say, and yes it is
There after all, into being
Brought by this careless act,
To instantly existing:
A sudden contradiction!
A wedding <u>with</u> a ring.
The possibilities are endless,
Just like a piece of string.

When I Am Gone

When I am gone,
You'll think no more of me,
Less even than you would
Of pigeons in a tree —

Days of pain there were,
And pleasure — weren't there three?
But I'll have my revenge,
And enjoy a glass or two;
At least I hope I can up there,
As I think no more of you!

Wise Old Birds

Do not ask for reasons,
Though I can give you one,
Why cockerels crow at break of day,
When first appears the sun.

'Tis buried deep my child, within,
And theories run amok,
Of ancient knowledge handed down
In the tongue that's known as Cluck.

A normal mortal cannot know
The wisdom of such birds —
Which see the world sail blithely on,
On the billows of its words.

Spoken words, that is to say,
In languages of men,
For Cluck was never one of these,
Nor written with a pen.

And it reflects the world of facts,
Though from a misted glass,
But to those who can decode it,
It's clear as burnished brass.

And I have studied hard and long,
And taken pains, it's true,
To comprehend the meaning of
A 'cock a doodle do'.

By candlelight or clear bright day,
I have found my true vocation:
To understand a rooster's brain,
In every complication.

Such study is, I'll tell you now,
Repaid a thousand times,
While all we humans struggle so,
To justify our crimes.

For mankind's words have caused our plight,
It's been revealed to me:
They've fed the flames of human greed,
Though we'll be swamped by sea.

The world is coming to an end
My child, I'm sad to say;
Your children face a harder task,
Or let it go astray.

The birds though have it on their minds;
They know just what to do.
They're telling us in terms of Cluck;
It's: 'cock a doodle do'.

Though what they're really saying is,
As many others won't,
It's not in fact that way at all,
But: 'cock a doodle don't'.

Flowers

'Oh, flowers will die,
And quickly too,
If false love you swear,
And in the case of last resort,
Expire in tears,
Before they're bought'.

'Yes, flowers may die,
But love will not,
If true love you give,
And for the finest love of all,
The blooms may live,
And never pall'.

"Ah, flowers may say
What you cannot,
In your lady's bower,
But love that's given in that way,
Is love of flowers,
For just a day."

"For love and flowers
Do not connect:
Love is made of grit and sweat,
And wrench and blood each inch,
Tinged with sweet regret —
A kiss with every pinch".

"Pretty flowers
Make a fine display,
Then with the wind, are gone;
As for flowers that do not die,
You have none,
And nor do I".

Brooklyn

I think I've been to Brooklyn,
And passed through Prospect Park,
And maybe Coney Island too,
But my memory is dark.

Mostly it was concrete,
So cold and wet and flat,
A million cars and people
Were all I saw, and that
Was my time in Brooklyn,
As I wrote it in my hat.

It was so long ago though,
And memories assert
A thousand wild chimera,
The mind cannot convert;
But the man in the corner surely,
Was real as New York dirt.

And yet, and yet I wonder —
My diary tells a tale,
Not written in my writing,
And maybe in a gale;
It carries strange accounting,
That's quite beyond the pale.

So did I go to Brooklyn?
I wonder now and stare
Through rain-flecked windows in
The train. Was I ever there?
Then a voice, American,
Was borne on smoke-filled air.

'Please return my hat', it said,
'I now have little hair.
I lost it in a fearsome fight
With a mauling grizzly bear,
And many months have passed, my
Friend, since I was oh so fair'.

'I have travelled wide and far,
But tracked you down with care,
Through bog and briar and bramble,
In the sun's ferocious glare.
When frozen darkness told me 'no',
I pressed on, au contraire'.

'Sometimes it was much to bear,
Only human as we are,
Though often, under darkened skies,
My wounds healed from afar,
As I sensed the angel's kiss
That glows to light each star'.

'I never lost my hope, you see,
Even without prayer,
As I followed you from Brooklyn,
Though you were never there'.

About Us

Dick Dixon

Dick Dixon was born in Sawbridgeworth, Hertfordshire; he works as a teacher at a college on the south coast of England. While at school, he won the Ilott prize for poetry in 1962. He graduated in mathematics in 1970 from the University of Wales, as it was then, and embarked on a rather chequered career, involving an insurance company, a British Rail drawing office, and various other ventures.

Eventually, light appeared at the end of the tunnel, and he realised that the answer surely was to engage in the teaching of mathematics, (though the precise nature of the question has remained obscure).

Recently, in 2013, he met Reine Mazoyer, the French artist, and it became quite clear quite quickly that together, they would have to write their book 'Rhymes for no Reason' together, after which it seemed churlish not to continue with 'Rhymes of the Newfangled Mariner', the present volume. In this book we hope you will be able to detect something of interest, or find a little something to amuse you when the cold inhospitable world has failed to come up with the goods!

Reine Mazoyer

Reine Mazoyer is a French artist. She was born in Montbrison in southern France and graduated from the 'Ecole des Beaux-Arts' at Saint-Etienne in 1965.

She married Robert Mazoyer (who died in 1999), the well-known movie-film director, and worked with him as art director. Later she worked as a director for documentary movies. She exhibits her art creations regularly in Europe and the United States.

Reine received the honour of 'Chevalier des Arts et des Lettres' in 2008.

After having written and illustrated two books herself, Reine met Dick Dixon, and together they realised that they were definitely crazy enough to create 'Rhymes of the Newfangled Mariner', having previously honed their skills in writing and illustrating 'Rhymes for no Reason'.

Dick Dixon and Reine Mazoyer at the Book Stop café in Eymet, France, in July 2016.

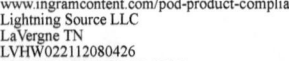